WORLD MUSIC DRUMMING
NEW ENSEMBLES AND SONGS

BY WILL SCHMID

A CROSS-CULTURAL CURRICULAR SUPPLEMENT

ISBN 978-0-634-08392-1

HAL•LEONARD®

Copyright © 2004 by HAL LEONARD LLC
International Copyright Secured   All Rights Reserved

BoVisit Hal Leonard Online at
www.halleonard.com

Contact Us:
Hal Leonard
7777 West Bluemound Road
Milwaukee, WI 53213
Email: info@halleonard.com

In Europe contact:
Hal Leonard Europe Limited
42 Wigmore Street
Marylebone, London, W1U 2RN
Email: info@halleonardeurope.com

In Australia contact:
Hal Leonard Australia Pty. Ltd.
4 Lentara Court
Cheltenham, Victoria, 3192 Australia
Email: info@halleonard.com.au

DIGITAL DOWNLOAD CODE
To access AUDIO MP3s, go to:
www.halleonard.com/mylibrary

3502-7593-7921-4582

Table of Contents

HOW TO ACCESS DIGITAL RECORDINGS

1. To access content in Hal Leonard's MY LIBRARY, go to **www.halleonard.com/mylibrary**.

2. Follow the instructions to set up your own My Library account, so that codes are saved for future access, and you don't have to re-enter them every time.

3. Once you have created your own library account, then enter the 16-digit product code listed on page 1.

4. **Important:** Follow the instructions on the "Read Me First" PDFs for Mac and PC to **properly** download, unzip, open and use these digital files.

About the Author

Will Schmid is past president of the 100,000-member MENC: The National Association for Music Education and professor emeritus at the University of Wisconsin–Milwaukee. He holds a B.A. from Luther College and a Ph.D. from the Eastman School of Music. Will is a program author for Pearson Scott Foresman's 2002 and 2005 *Silver Burdett Making Music* series. He is the principal author of the best selling *Hal Leonard Guitar Method* (in ten languages) and over sixty other books/CDs/DVDs for guitar, banjo, and strings. Dr. Schmid is also the principal author/editor of an 8-volume high school choral textbook, *Something New to Sing About* (Glencoe/G. Schirmer) and a student text and teacher's guide entitled *A Vision Shared: A Tribute to Woody Guthrie and Leadbelly* (MENC). He has given workshops throughout the United States and in Australia, Canada, Japan, Mexico and Europe. After a two-year $ 140,000 national pilot project in twenty schools nationwide, Dr. Schmid launched the *World Music Drumming* curriculum which brings the excitement of African and Latin drumming and singing to schools throughout the world.

Will Schmid

Dr. Schmid is the recipient of the 1996 Distinguished Alumnus Award from the Eastman School of Music. In 2002 he was named a Lowell Mason Fellow by MENC and given the Distinguished Service Award from the Music Industry Conference (MIC).

During his presidency of MENC (1994-96), Dr. Schmid worked to reestablish the importance of active music making in schools and in America at large. MENC created new partnership initiatives in the areas of guitar, keyboards, strings, drumming, and singing as exemplified by the *Get America Singing . . . Again!* Campaign and the GAMA/NAMM/MENC-sponsored Teaching Guitar workshops in operation since 1995.

About World Music Drumming

The World Music Drumming Pilot Project

In the spring of 1996 I began an eighteen-month pilot project primarily funded by REMO, Inc. which addressed the following goals:

- Bring the excitement of world music and drumming to middle school (and grades 3-5, 9-12) curriculums
- Teach African and Latin-American culture
- Build important work and community skills:
  - communication and listening
  - cooperative teamwork
  - respect for others

To accomplish these goals, the project set out to:

- Develop a 30-lesson curriculum for middle school general music classes that works in:
  - 6- or 9-week units (wheel)
  - 9- to 18-week A/B day structures
- Establish strong connections with other subjects
- Use the excitement and motivation of drumming from Africa and the Caribbean
- Engage students through an active, hands-on approach

In the first twelve months (1996-97), five middle school teachers and project assistant Sheila Feay-Shaw from the Milwaukee Public Schools worked with me to develop the thirty-lesson curriculum. During the fall and spring semesters of that school year, the team of teachers and I met weekly to work out and edit the first draft of the thirty-lesson curriculum. Special stakeholder sessions were held with school administrators, parents, teachers of other subjects in the schools, and school support staff such as guidance counselors, curriculum specialists, and assistant principals (discipline).

In the summer of 1997, fifteen additional pilot teachers and schools were chosen from throughout the United States and Canada. Every attempt was made to pick schools with different socio-economic profiles including inner city, suburban, mid-size city and small city/rural. These fifteen new teachers plus the five original Milwaukee teachers attended a week-long training workshop in Lake Geneva, Wisconsin taught by Ghanaian master drummer, Sowah Mensah and myself. The extended group of twenty pilot teachers continued to teach and help refine the *World Music Drumming* curriculum throughout that school year.

National Music Standards

In all phases of this project, there has been a strong focus on how *World Music Drumming* could help students meet the *National Music Standards* — now adopted or modified and in use in most states in the United States. Most of these standards are threaded through the curriculum.

Developments Since 1998

In 1998 Hal Leonard Corporation published the *World Music Drumming* publications — The 96pp *Teacher's Book*, the *Cross-Cultural Student Enrichment Book* and *Video*. Those publications still form the basis of the curriculum that serves as a foundation for this book/CD.

Developments in *World Music Drumming* since 1998 include:

- In addition to the original grades 6-8 target population of students, the curriculum is now being widely taught in grades 3-5, in high schools, and in community-based programs.
- The curriculum has also been published and enhanced with additional cultures, recordings, ensembles and songs in *Silver Burdett Making Music 2005*, Grades 6, 7, and 8 (Pearson Scott Foresman).
- Choral and band programs are performing *World Music Drumming* arrangements.
- Churches, synagogues, and other spiritual centers are using *World Music Drumming* with singing in their celebrations.
- *World Music Drumming* is now being taught in thousands of schools throughout the United States, Canada, and other countries.
- Workshop teaching staff members Paul Corbiere, Margaret Jerz, James Mader, and Anne Fennell have published or are working on auxiliary publications.
- The *World Music Drumming* summer workshops have expanded to multiple sites each summer serving hundreds of teachers, guidance counselors, spiritual leaders, and recreation specialists. More information on the summer workshops is available on page 48.

Visit our website at: *www.worldmusicdrumming.com*

How To Use This Book/Audio Access

Teaching Guidelines

The basis for this curricular supplement is clearly developed in the *World Music Drumming* publications — The 96pp *Teacher's Book*, the *Cross-Cultural Student Enrichment Book* and *Video*.

Following are some teaching guidelines that should help you teach the ensembles and songs in this collection to various populations.

- **Teach orally/aurally** in the style of master drummers and teachers like Sowah Mensah (see summer workshops, p. 48). Music learned this way is perceived as an integrated whole.
- **Teach by example with few words.** We all have a tendency to talk way too much when we teach.
- **Vocalize drumming patterns** with pitch inflections as you play and teach, and ask students to do the same. This multi-modal teaching is a very old and wonderful idea that helps people learn faster and remember longer.
- **Repeat, repeat, repeat.** It takes many repetitions to deeply learn rhythms and songs.
- **Aim for success,** and do not take on more than your students can handle. Playing a simple ensemble or part of an ensemble well is a much more powerful experience than playing a difficult piece poorly.
- **Movement is the cure for most rhythmic ills.** When people are not feeling the rhythms together, get them up and have them move until they are feeling rhythms through their whole body.
- **Teach all the parts to all the people.** They will learn to listen and react to other instruments best when they have played all parts.
- **Everyone is a singer and dancer.** Assume that students will get into it if you feel comfortable singing and moving. Drumming can be a useful back door to singing for those who may not see themselves as "singers." The models for this are everywhere in the cultures and styles of music you are playing.
- **Teach good technique** every day. Teaching proper posture and hand positions shows respect for the traditions and communicates a high standard as the only acceptable alternative.

- **Bring your best musicianship** to bear on all you and your students do with drumming and singing. Concepts such as balance, blend, intonation, phrasing and ensemble unity should apply every time you play.
- **Ask questions** such as:
  – "How is the balance?"
  – "Can you hear the other parts?"
  – "What can we do to improve?"
- **Encourage teamwork** by asking students to work together and help each other.
- **Reinforce the keywords** such as *respect, unity, listen, teamwork, focus,* etc. from the original *World Music Drumming Teacher's Book*. Put posters on your wall that reinforce these ideas.
- **Share the joy** of World Music Drumming with stakeholders such as parents, administrators, other teachers/co-workers. Let students do the teaching and demonstrating. No school board member can refuse a child's invitation to drum.
- **Invite guests** from outside your school to share their musical or cultural expertise.
- **Keep learning new things yourself.** The best model for students is a teacher that is still learning. Attend a summer workshop (p. 48).
- **Encourage soloists** to volunteer to play over the top of many of the ensembles in this book.
- **Ask students to create** their own pieces. They will enjoy this a great deal, and it will spawn a whole new way of programming.
- **Use other musical resources** to enhance drumming. Add instruments such as guitars, electric bass, keyboards, or flutes.
- **Use the Audio Recordings** for playalongs and as a model.
- **Play around** with the pieces. Try new ways of doing things by:
  – Changing instrumentation
  – Varying the tempo
  – Adding solos or extra parts
  – Making up your own ending signals
  – Trying new hybrids that cross over styles

Keep observing what the best *World Music Drumming* teachers do, and emulate those models.

Above all — have fun!

willschmid@aol.com

Desert Fire

Will Schmid

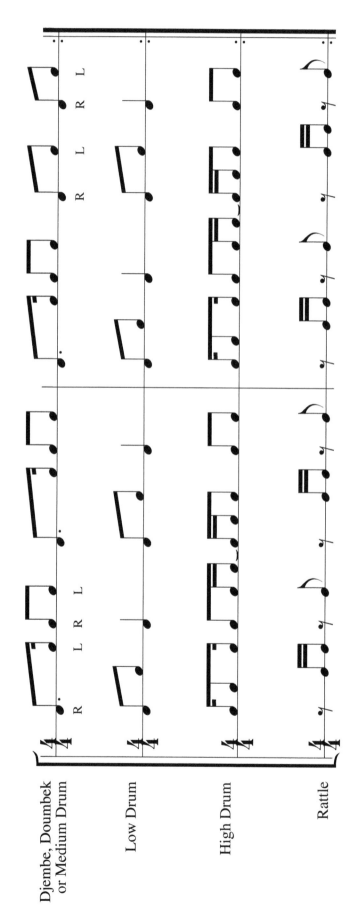

Djembe, Doumbek or Medium Drum

Low Drum

High Drum

Rattle

Leader Drum
Ending Signal

Learning Sequence for Desert Fire

- Djembe, Doumbek or Medium Drum
  - This is the key to this Middle-Eastern sounding ensemble. Teach all students to play it until they know it well. It should be louder than the other parts.
  - The doumbek *(doom-bek)* and the djembe *(gem-bay)* are both goblet-shaped drums with a deep bass (low) tone in the center and a sharp-sounding open (high) tone. The darabuka *(dahr-a-boo-ka)* is another name for a drum similar to the doumbek. The doumbek gets its name from the low tone *(doum)* and high tone *(bek).* Traditional doumbeks are made of ceramic or silver.
- Low Drum
  - The Low Drum part should be softer than the Medium Drum part. Its role is to support the Medium Drum part. If students cannot hear the Medium Drum part, they are playing too loud.
- High Drum
  - The High Drum part is like a filagree ornamental part that should be played lightly and not dominate.
- Rattle
  - Play it against either a hand or a leg for a dry sound. If shekeres have loose netting, gather some in the hand to tighten up the sound.

Doumbek

Singing "A Ram Sam Sam"

- The traditional Moroccan round, "A Ram Sam Sam," is a natural combination with *Desert Fire.*
- Have students pronounce the word "ram" and "sam" with an *(ah)* sound. The word "guli" should be pronounced *(goo-lee).*
- These words have no specific meaning.
- Begin with the drums; add the song to the ensemble; have the drums play an interlude; then bring back the song.

A Ram Sam Sam

traditional round from Morocco

A ram sam sam a ram sam sam, gu-li gu-li gu-li gu-li gu-li ram sam sam,

A ra-fi a ra-fi, gu-li gu-li gu-li gu-li gu-li ram sam sam.

Supplementary Strategies for Desert Fire

- Sing and dance John Krumm's round, "Dance for the Nations," in *Rounds Galore* by Sol Weber (Astoria) or in *Silver Burdett Making Music,* grade 6.
- Play *Desert Fire* with selections from *Arabic Groove* (Putumayo, PUT-189-2)
  - #3 "Leiley" performed by Dania from Lebanon.
  - #10 "Ne Me Jugez Pas" performed by Sawt El Atlas from Morocco.

On the Mountain

Will Schmid

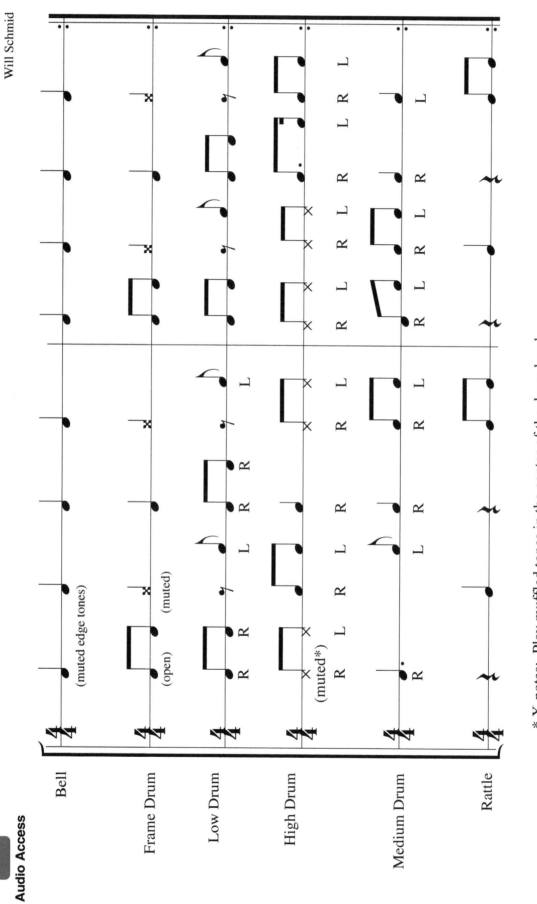

Bell

Frame Drum

Low Drum

High Drum

Medium Drum

Rattle

Audio Access

* X-notes: Play muffled tones in the center of the drum head.
Let the whole palm fall quietly to the head without bouncing.

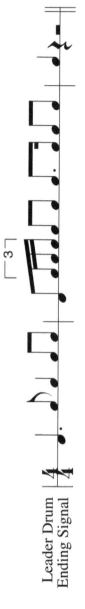

Leader Drum
Ending Signal

Learning Sequence for On the Mountain

- Medium Drum
  - Begin by teaching everyone the Medium Drum part that is the heart of this ensemble. Pay particular attention to the right- and left-hand patterns.
  - You may wish to teach the melody to "Sow It On the Mountain" and challenge students to play the Medium Drum part while singing the melody. During this stage, it may help to pitch the melody in a lower key such as D major.
- Low Drum
  - The Low Drum part uses a repeated right hand in the middle of the drum head to achieve a consistent sound. When students can play the Medium and Low Drum parts with ease, put them together.
- High Drum
  - The High Drum uses a muted-hand technique to play muffled tones (X-note heads) in the center of the drum head. Ask students to hold their relaxed hands about two inches above the center of the head; then let the hands fall without bouncing. It may help to call these muffled tones "mittens" as a way of emphasizing they they should be soft and muffled. Practice a series of muted tones with alternating hands.

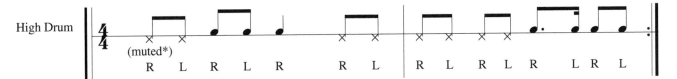

  - The open tones should stand out while the muted tones should barely be heard. Watch out for those who bounce on the muted low tones and therefore play them much too loud.
  - Have students verbalize the sound of this part as they practice. Multi-modal learning like this is very traditional in many cultures and helps speed the learning process. Try: "mitten da-da-dat, mitten mitten mitten dat-da-da-da." Inflect the pitch of the voice to reflect the low or high tones. Whisper the word, "mitten."
  - Point out how complementary this part is with the other drum parts.
- Frame Drum
  - Play the muted X-tone in center of the head without lifting the hand.
- Putting it all together. Add the parts in score order. Listen for balance.

Singing "Sow It On the Mountain"

- Teach the melody by ear until all can sing it with ease.
- Add the other parts in this order (Tenor, Alto, Bass) if these voices are available. The song sounds good with two, three, or four parts.
- You may wish to feature solos or small groups on some verses.
- Consider singing sections unaccompanied; then bring the drums back in.
- Add instruments such as guitars, piano, bass, autoharp, etc.

Supplementary Strategies for On the Mountain

- Play *On the Mountain* with the Temptations hit, "My Girl" written by Smokey Robinson.
- Research The Carter Family, one of the two pioneer singing acts of country music. Their original lyrics and melody were quite different from this arrangement of "Sow It On the Mountain."

Sow It On the Mountain

The Carter Family

Arranged at the Stringalong Weekend
by Ann and Will Schmid, P. Hambleton, M. Larsen

1. If you're feelin' weary, won't you lend a hand to someone? (3 times)
   You're gonna reap just what you sow. CHORUS

2. If you're feelin' hungry, won't you share your bread with someone? (3 times)
   You're gonna reap just what you sow. CHORUS

3. If you're feelin' lonely, won't you be a friend to someone? (3 times)
   You're gonna reap just what you sow. CHORUS

Drum Up the Sun

Will Schmid

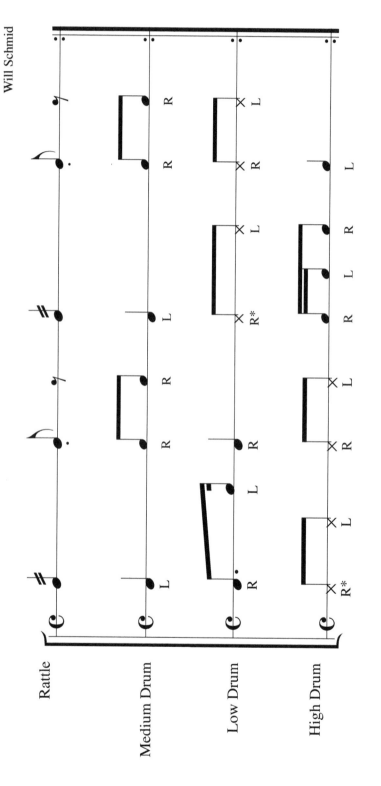

*Notes with "X" heads should be played with a muffled palm stroke in the middle of the drum. If the Rattle part is played using a shekere, put the beaded end in your palm and rotate the handle to create the sound on beats 1 and 3; then stop abruptly on beats 2 and 4.

Learning Sequence for Drum Up the Sun

- Set the Stage
  - Ask students to imagine themselves on the desert just before dawn. Their role as drummers is to drum up the sun. It will only rise if they play well.
- Rattle
  - See instructions under ensemble. This should sound like a rattlesnake.
- Medium Drum
  - Play softly so as not to scare the sun from coming up.
- Low Drum and High Drum
  - Both the Low and High Drum parts use a muted-hand technique. See the muffled tone exercises on page 9.

Singing "Sahara Sunrise"

- This song, sung as a vocal exercise by a theatre group on the Sahara Desert, uses neutral syllables without specific meaning to vocalize in a style similar to chant. Strive for pure "ah" and "oo" vowels throughout.
- Sing once in unison; then sing twice as a four-part round. Have each part keep singing the last line at the end until all parts are singing in unison.
- A light guitar accompaniment may be used on the Am chord.

Sahara Sunrise
Four-part Round

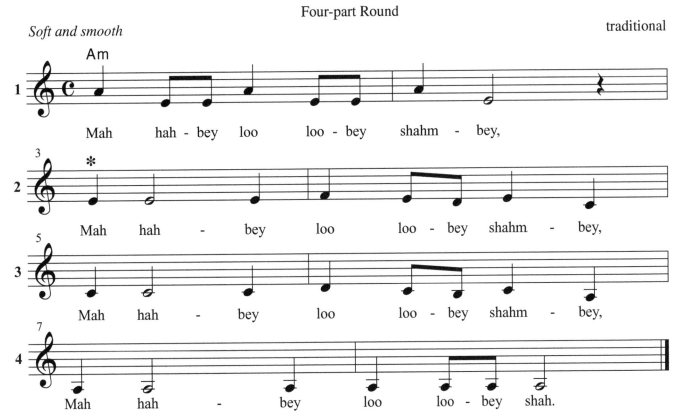

* The next part of the round enters when the previous part reaches this line.

Supplementary Strategies for Drum Up the Sun/Sahara Sunrise

- Play alto recorders on "Sahara Sunrise" with singing and as an interlude.
- *Drum Up the Sun* can also be played with "Kum Ba Yah" sung in 4/4 time.

Motormind

Will Schmid

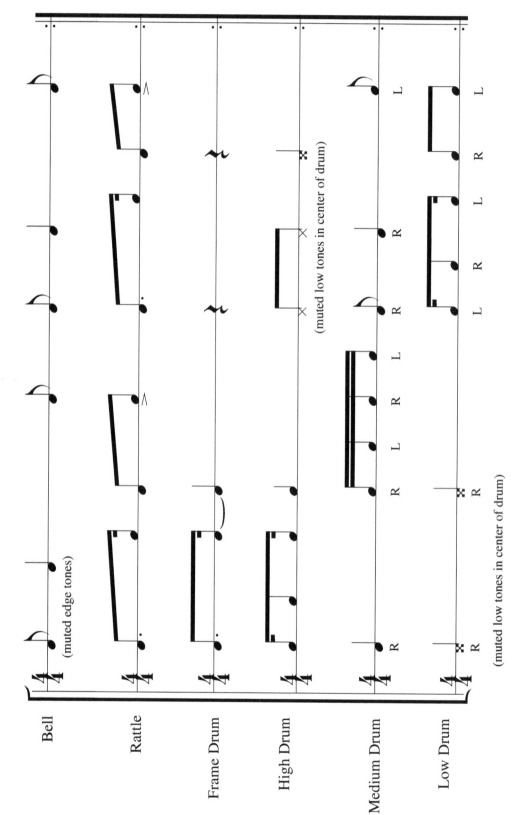

Learning Sequence for Motormind

- *Motormind* packs the speed and the energy of an electronic video game (or the mind of middle-level student).
  - Ask students to imagine a video game where they are chasing a speeding convertible and trying to jump in at high speed. To do so, the chase car would have to get up to the speed of the convertible before they could jump in. Coming in with a new part in a drum ensemble works just like that — you have to be *up to speed* mentally before starting to play.
- Bell
  - Play with a wooden stick on the open edge of the bell. Hold the bell firmly to mute it.
- Rattle
  - Alternate between the thigh and hand, accenting on the second and fourth upbeats. This rhythm is the same as the rattle rhythm for *Gahu* (Ghanaian piece) except that the up-down directions are different.
- Frame Drum
  - Larger and lower frame drums work best for this part. Play open tones about one-third of the distance from the edge of the head. Mute the drum head on beats three and four.
- High Drum
  - The High Drum starts on beat one; then the Medium Drum emphasizes beat two and passes it on to the Low Drum on beat three. The muted tones serve as time keepers and will not be heard.
- Medium Drum
  - Play out on beat two. Notice the R-L hand indications. Feel free to reverse the right and left hands.
- Low Drum
  - Keep time with muted low tones on beats one and two; then bring out the third and fourth beats as open tones.
- Putting it all together
  - Practice the Rattle and Frame Drum together. If the Frame Drums are late on their second hit, have them practice playing the Rattle part and verbalizing their Frame Drum part to coincide with the Rattle's upstroke.
  - Practice the High, Medium, and Low Drum parts together slowly at first. Have students listen for the movement of energy from part to part.

Supplementary Strategies for Motormind

- Play the ensemble with sticks instead of with hands. Sticks give the ensemble a much more "in-your-face" sound. Sticks are commonly used in West African drumming.
- Listen to how modern drummers play cascading patterns on a drumset that move from tom-tom to tom-tom.
- Have students find playalong recordings that work with *Motormind*.
- Ask students to break into Rhythm Complement groups with a High, Medium, and Low Drum in each group.
  - Have them create patterns that move from drum to drum as they do in *Motormind*.

Tuning Tip

- *Start by tuning the Medium (12") Drums to a unison pitch somewhere in the middle of the spectrum.*
- *Next tune the High Drums around a perfect fourth higher.*
- *Tune the Low Drums a fourth lower.*
- *Tuning in fourths avoids common chordal sounds.*

Dowel Drumsticks

- *You can make your own drumsticks by going to a lumber retailer and buying 1/4" or 3/8" dowels and cutting them to one-foot lengths.*
- *Sand the ends of the sticks to save drum heads.*
- *Paint the end of the sticks held in hand to distinguish them from bell sticks which get all chewed up.*

Harambee

Will Schmid

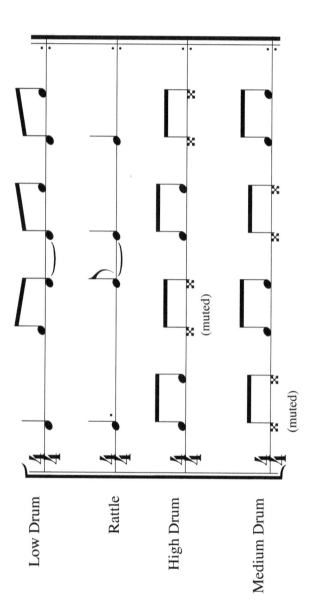

Learning Sequence for Harambee

- Discuss
  - *Harambee* is a Swahili word which means "We all pull (or push) together." Discuss with students the implications of this concept for the United States and the rest of the world today.
- High Drum and Medium Drum
  - These two complementary parts weave the background fabric.
- Low Drum
  - Assign one hand to the low tone and the other to the high tone.
- Rattle
  - Hit against the hand or thigh.

Singing "Get It Together"

- The *Call* may be sung by either a soloist or a section. Get the audience to join in on the *Response*.
- Drumming interludes featuring drum soloists over the top of the ensemble may be used after some of the Refrains.
- Power chords (C5 and Bb5) are given to the right.

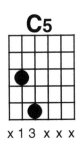

C5

x 1 3 x x x

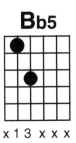

Bb5

x 1 3 x x x

Get It Together

Will Schmid

* "Harambee" is a Swahili word which means: "We all pull (or push) together."

2. Tell the people, Harambee, . . .
3. Love one another, Harambee, . . .
4. Tap the power, Harambee, . . .

Verses 5 plus: Make up your own lyrics.

Supplementary Strategies for Harambee/Get It Together

- These pieces can be used to celebrate Kwanzaa (December).
- Ask students to brainstorm new verses.

Peace Drum Song

3-part song or round

Will Schmid

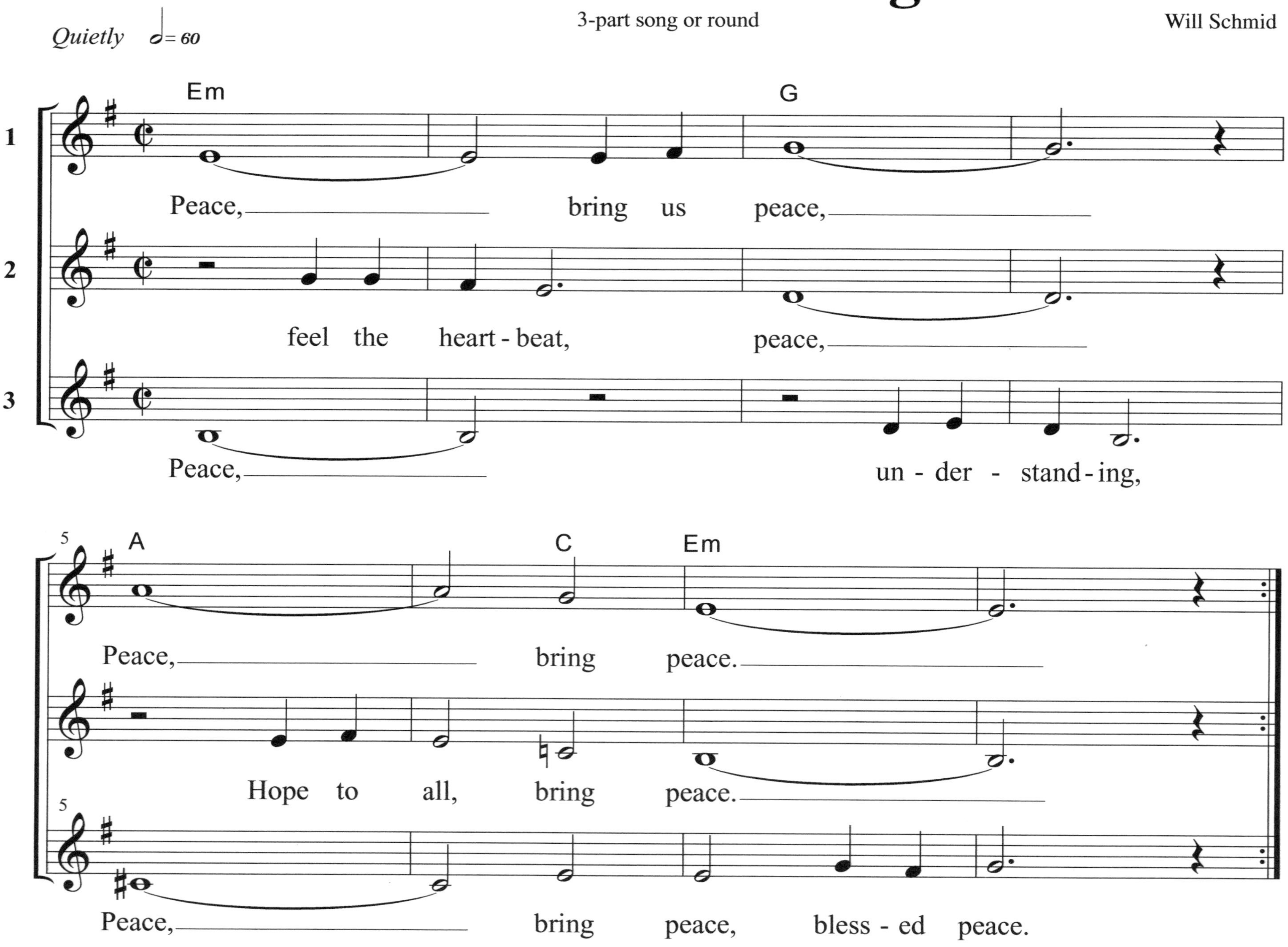

Audio Access

Quietly $\quad \circ = 60$

Peace,_____ bring us peace,_____

feel the heart - beat, peace,_____

Peace,_____ un - der - stand - ing,

Peace,_____ Hope to all, bring peace._____

Peace,_____ bring peace._____

Peace,_____ bring peace, bless - ed peace.

Learning Sequence for Peace Drum

- Background
  - The "Peace Drum Song" and *Peace Drum* ensemble was written as a response to the New York World Trade Center tragedy of 9-11-2001. Use the words of the song to discuss current peace issues with your students.
- Low Drum
  - This is the "heartbeat" of the song in the sense that Native Americans use that word to describe their drumming. It may be played with one hand in the center of the drum head or you may use a padded stick/mallet. Imagine a Plains Indian ceremonial drum with several players around the drum playing the same part with cattail-shaped drum sticks.
- Low Frame Drum or Bass Drum
  - This should be as low a tone as possible and can be played with hand or padded mallet.
- Rattle
  - Hit against the hand and accent the first and third hits.
- Combining Parts
  - Give students the fun challenge of play both drum parts at once.

Peace Drum

Will Schmid

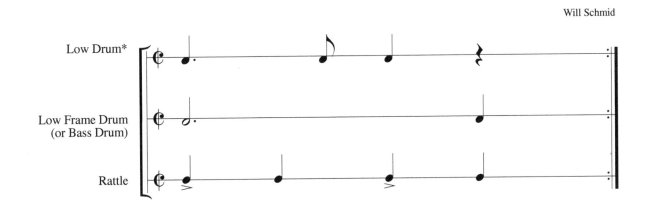

Singing "Peace Drum Song"

- Start the drumming; then add the optional guiar part.
- In unison sing line 1 (two staves), then line 2, then line 3.
- Then sing the three-part round twice followed by line 1 until everyone is singing quietly in unison. End by singing line 1 as softly as possible.
- If you wish to involve the audience teach them line 1 and have them continue singing it softly throughout.

Supplementary Strategies for Peace Drum

- Double the singing parts with soft instruments like alto recorders
- Make a "Peace" bulletin board by having students contribute things that are related to peace issues.
- Find and sing other peace songs such as "Peace Like a River," Jean Ritchie's "Peace Round," or Tom Paxton's "Peace Will Come."

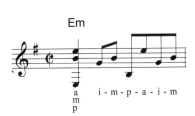

Fingerstyle Guitar Part

Rock It!

Will Schmid

Audio Access

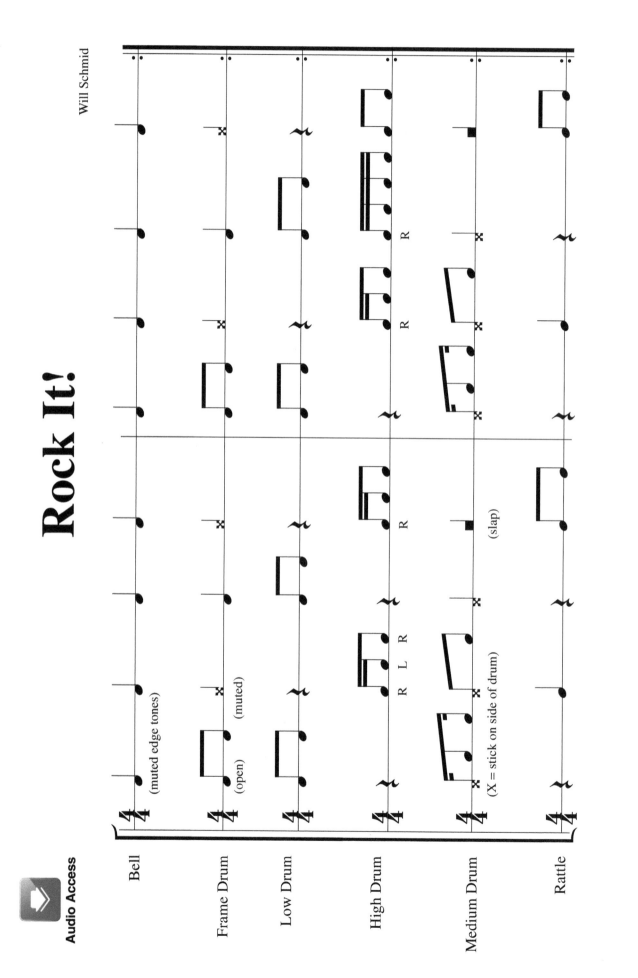

▦ Learning Sequence for Rock It!

- Background
  - *Rock It!* has the straight-up, squared-off rock sound typified by even eighth notes. In the late 1950s and '60s, the basic drum beat moved away from the triplet-feel swing beat and headed toward the even-eighth style found in *Rock It!* This change in drum beat signalled the move from "rock & roll" to "rock." Teach *Rock It!* as a contrast to *Swing It*, the piece which follows. See Supplemetary Strategies below for more ideas.

- Medium Drum
  - Teach this part first, because it is the most important and trickiest part.
  - Start by having everyone practice the part on their thighs.
  - Begin with the left-hand stick part (hands only) hit on the left thigh.
  - Add the right hand open tones on the other thigh.
  - Finally add the right-hand slap on the right thigh by accenting and keeping the hand from bouncing off the thigh. The slap is a fairly complex drum stroke that takes time to master. What you may want to do here is to do a "fake slap" which hits an accented open tone without letting the hand bounce off the drum head.
  - Transfer this to the drum using stick and hand.

- Frame Drum and Low Drum
  - These two drums work together to create the sound of a basic rock drum set. Point out that the Frame Drum muted sound in the middle of the drum is like the snare drum rim shot and should be accented. The mistake that many students make is to lift their hand on the mute.
  - The Low Drum part should use only one hand.

- High Drum
  - This part is complementary to the Low Drum part. Practice them together to establish an even alternation. Some talented student will probably volunteer to play both parts — which works except for the ending.

- Rattle
  - Hit against the hand or thigh.

- Combining Parts
  - Bring in the parts in score order two measures apart.

- Solos: This piece practically begs for soloists to play over the top of the ensemble.
  - Solo drums should be able to cut through or ride over the top of the ensemble sound. Djembes work well because of their sharp tone quality, and high drums played with sticks also cut through.
  - Create a way for soloists to volunteer — perhaps setting up a high drum with sticks and encouraging students to come up and play.

James Mader and students, Ft. Lauderdale, Florida

❖ Supplementary Strategies for Rock It!

- Engage students in the process of finding classic rock recordings that work with *Rock It!*
- Because the early rock & roll artists (1955-58) such as Elvis Presley and Fats Domino were essentially doing an updated version of rhythm & blues, the predominant rhythms were the triplet swing feel or shuffle. Artists such as Little Richard and Chuck Berry helped move the beat to even eighth notes.

Swing It

Will Schmid

Light and Subtle

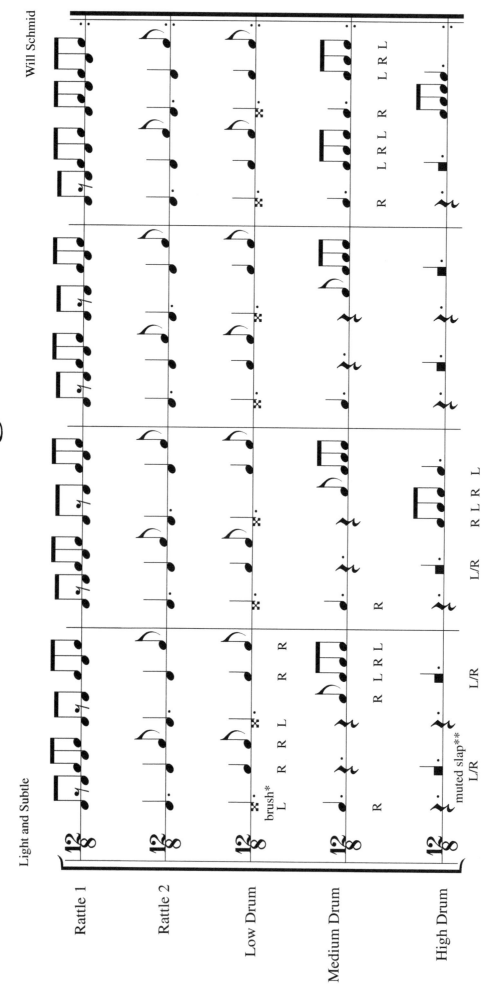

Rattle 1

Rattle 2

Low Drum

brush*
L R R L   R R

Medium Drum

R   R L R L   R

High Drum

muted slap**
L/R   L/R   L/R   R L R L   L R L

Leader Drum
Ending Signal

* Brush across the drum head with the left hand to imitate the sound of a brush stroke on a snare drum.

** Lay the left hand lightly on the drum head while playing an open (high) tone with the right hand.

22

Learning Sequence for Swing It

- Background
  - *Swing It* is the triplet-feel opposite of *Rock It!* Think "subtle" on this one.
- Rattles
  - Use the Rattle 1 part to help students get the triplet feel.
  - Rattle 2 is the typical rhythm played by the drum set's ride cymbal.
- Low Drum
  - The Low Drum plays the same rhythm as Rattle 2. Practice the brush stroke on the drum head. The open tones should be very soft.
- Medium Drum and High Drum
  - To play the L/R slap in the High Drum part, lay the left hand lightly on the drum head while playing an open (high) tone with the right hand.
- Combining Parts
  - On some songs, you may wish to omit the Medium and High Drums.

> **Teacher Tip**
>
> *Get to know the four-bar structure by saying the measure numbers aloud as you play.*

Singing "Swing Low, Sweet Chariot"

- This classic African-American spiritual is an easy choice for practicing the swing rhythms. When students know the song by heart, see if they can sing it while playing the Rattle 2 and/or Low Drum parts.

Swing Low, Sweet Chariot

Swing eighth notes

African-American Spiritual

Supplementary Strategies for Swing It

- Play *Swing It* with other songs such as "Wimoweh," "Summertime," "Sentimental Journey," or any "Boogey Woogey."
- Play *Swing It* with the "Sometime, Somewhere Blues" which follows.

Sometime, Somewhere Blues

Music and lyrics
by Will Schmid

Audio Access

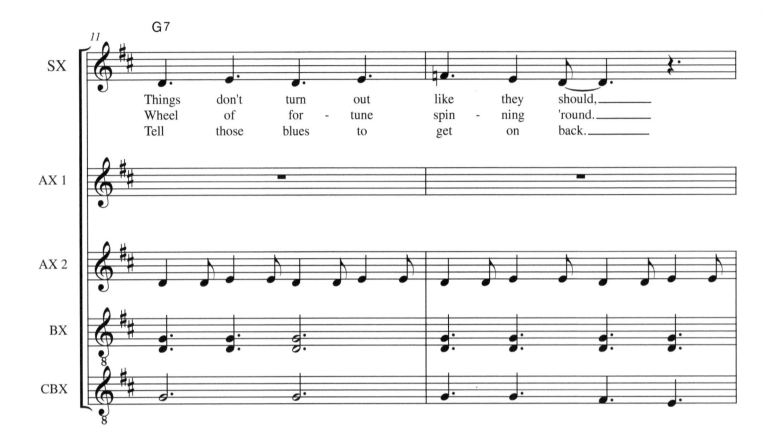

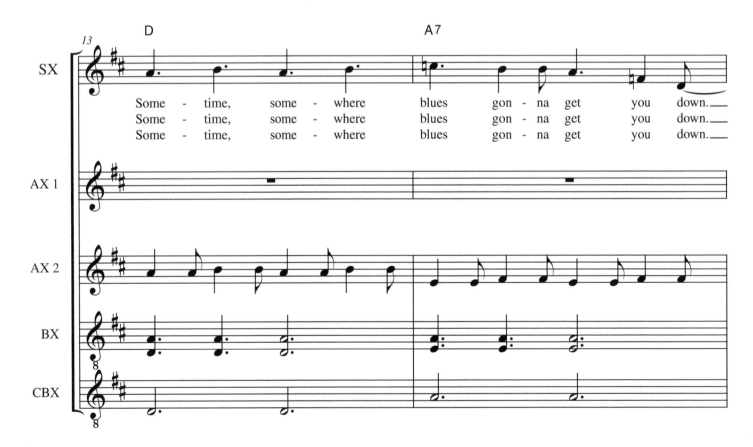

⬦ ⬦

⬛ Learning Sequence for Sometime, Somewhere Blues

- Discuss the nature of the blues style and how "Sometime, Somewhere Blues" is both similar to and different from other blues.
  - Similarities to other blues
    - Call (2-bar phrase) and response (2-bar answer) structure
    - Blue notes = lowered 7th (C-natural) and lowered 3rd (F-natural)
    - Shuffle or swing rhythm (triplet feel)
    - Typical blues lyrics about "hard times"
    - Solos use the blues pentatonic (D F G A C)
  - Differences from other basic blues
    - This is a 16-bar blues (instead of the more common 12-bar blues)
    - It is played by xylophones and drum ensemble rather than guitar, piano, bass, drumset.
- Bass Xylophone and Alto Xylophone 2 (Back-up parts on page 31)
  - Begin with these two parts because they form the basic *back-up* (as opposed to *lead*) part of the band. It might be helpful to have one or both of the Rattle parts from *Swing It* played by the other members of the ensemble to establish the triplet-feel shuffle rhythm. Play along with the CD when players are up to speed.
- Contrabass Xylophone (Back-up part on page 31)
  - If no Contrabass Xylophone bars are available, this part may be played on a Bass Xylophone. Another possibility is to double it or play it on an electric bass.
- Soprano Xylophone (Lead part on page 30)
  - Practice having the whole class play and sing the Soprano Xylophone part, which in blues terms is called the *lead*. Provide chordal accompaniment for the singing by having some players on Bass Xylophone and Alto Xylophone 2 as well as at least one Rattle player. Play and sing along with the CD.
- Alto Xylophone 1 (Response part on page 30)
  - This part should be played only after sung verses 1, 2, and 3.
  - Sing the Alto Xylophone 2 part an octave lower than notated. On the second response, the lower note would normally have been a C#, but since this pitch is not available on classroom xylophones, pitch A was chosen. Singers, however, could choose to sing C# and B instead of A and G.
  - Play along with the CD to get the syncopated feel of the tied notes.

Margaret Jerz and students, Schofield, Wisconsin

28

- Xylophone Solo Responses (improvised, not written out)
  – Improvised blues solos can be played by either Soprano Xylophone or Alto Xylophone.
  – Set up the solo instrument with the blues pentatonic (D F G A C)
  – The CD recording leaves the Alto Xylophone 1 (Response) open on the second and fourth time through. The solos can be played in these same spots.
  – The first and third response solos are played over a D chord, so base the solos on the note D using the F and C notes above and below.

sample solo

  – The second response solo is played over an A7 chord, so base the solo on the note A using the C and G notes above and below.

sample solo

  – Once students get the feel of the solos, they can branch out more.
  – Suggest that students "ride" the triplet rhythms on their solos.

▶ Singing and Playing Sometime, Somewhere Blues

- Back-up Instruments
  – *Swing It* back-up instruments should include both Rattle 1 and Rattle 2 as well as the Low Drum part. Including the other two drum parts is optional, because it runs the risk of sounding rather muddy.
  – Other back up instruments might include guitar and/or electric bass. If the guitarist plays with a capo at fret 5, the common blues shuffle pattern in A (sounds D) will work well with the back-up xylophones.
- Verse 1
  – Sing verse 1 and play all parts including the Alto Xylophone 1 (Response).
- Instrumental (second time through)
  – Play all parts, but Solo replaces the Alto Xylophone 1 (Response)
  – The three solo measures (3-4, 7-8, and 15-16) can either be played by one player or split up among three.
- Verse 2
  – Sing verse 2 and play all parts including the Alto Xylophone 1 (Response).
  – If the CD is not used, you may wish to sing (not play) the lead and response over the back-up xylophones.
- Instrumental (fourth time through)
  – Play all parts, but Solo replaces the Alto Xylophone 1 (Response)
- Verse 3
  – Sing verse 3 and play all parts including the Alto Xylophone 1 (Response).
- Option when CD is not used.
  – Play the blues solo (D pentatonic) in place of the regular melody on instrumentals.

◈ Supplementary Strategies for Sometime, Somewhere Blues

- Have students make up new verses.
- Compare this 16-bar blues form to 12-bar blues and 8-bar blues.

Sometime, Somewhere Blues

Soprano Xylophone (Lead)

Music and lyrics
by Will Schmid

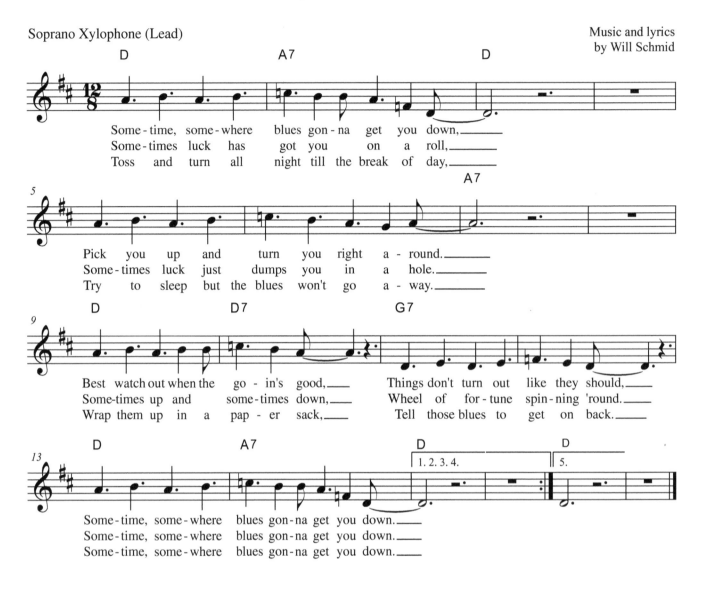

Some - time, some - where blues gon - na get you down,_____
Some - times luck has got you on a roll,_____
Toss and turn all night till the break of day,_____

Pick you up and turn you right a - round._____
Some - times luck just dumps you in a hole._____
Try to sleep but the blues won't go a - way._____

Best watch out when the go - in's good,____ Things don't turn out like they should,____
Some-times up and some-times down,____ Wheel of for - tune spin-ning 'round.____
Wrap them up in a pap - er sack,____ Tell those blues to get on back.____

Some - time, some - where blues gon-na get you down.____
Some - time, some - where blues gon-na get you down.____
Some - time, some - where blues gon-na get you down.____

Sometime, Somewhere Blues

Alto Xylophone (Response)

Music and lyrics
by Will Schmid

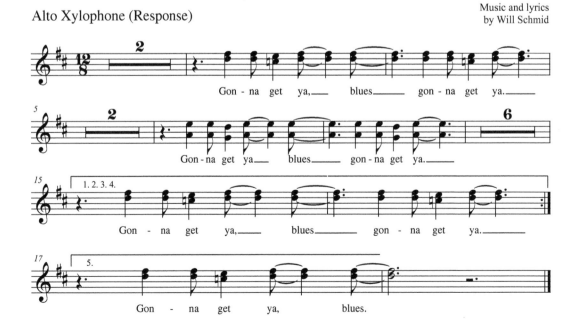

Gon - na get ya,____ blues____ gon - na get ya.____

Gon - na get ya____ blues____ gon - na get ya.____

Gon - na get ya,____ blues____ gon - na get ya.____

Gon - na get ya, blues.

30

Sometime, Somewhere Blues

Music and Lyrics
by Will Schmid

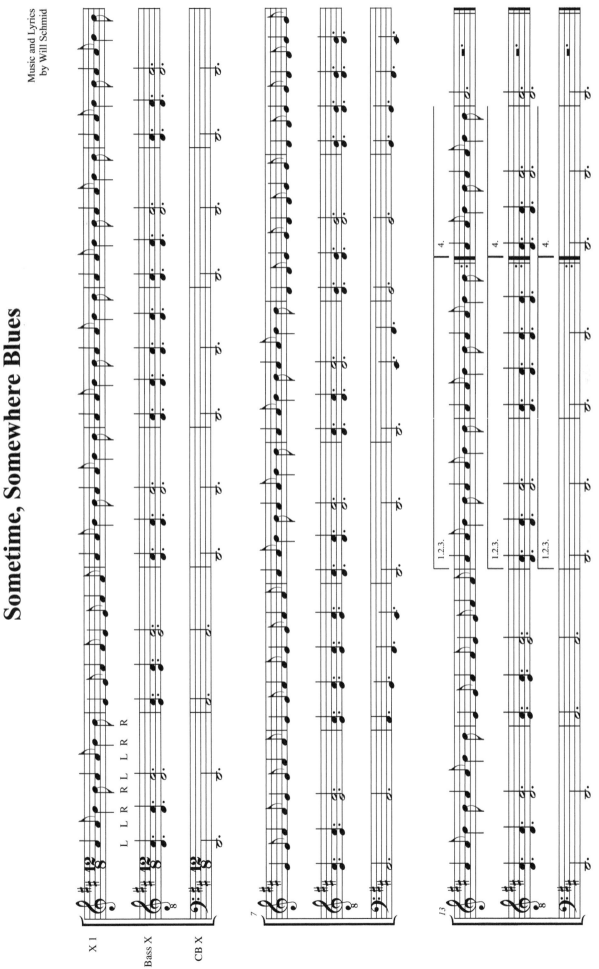

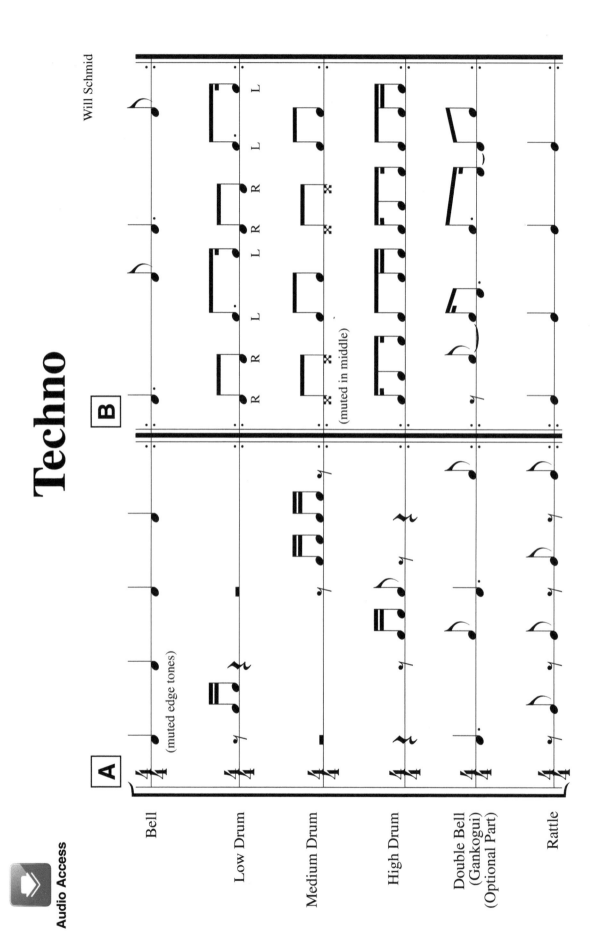

Techno

Will Schmid

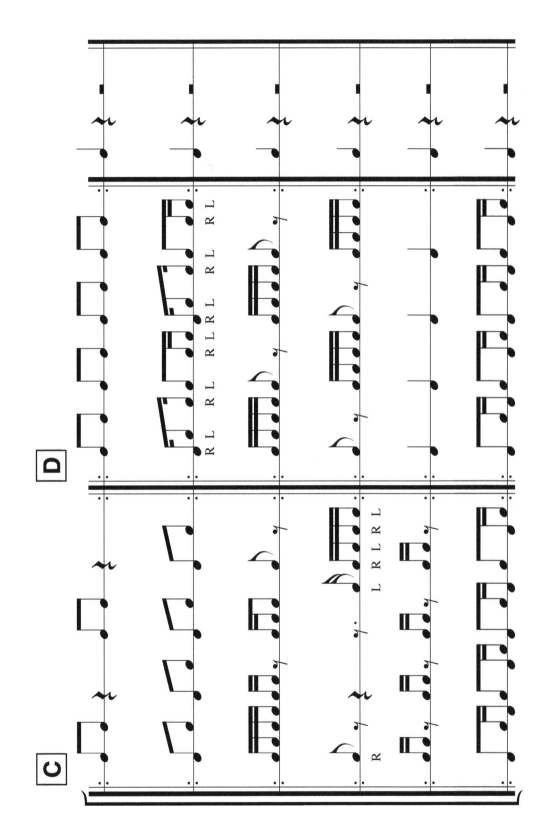

Learning Sequence for Techno

- Techno/electronica is a hard-driving dance style that grew out of disco. Playing this piece will require everyone's total attention.
  - *Techno* is divided into four sections.
  - The CD has two versions — a slower, practice tempo, and a fast tempo.
  - The ensemble is divided into two basic groups:
    - Back-up: Bell, Double Bell, Rattle
    - Drums: Low, Medium, High
  - *Techno* can be played with either hands or sticks. Start with hands; then try playing with sticks (1/4" dowels, 1 foot long). Playing with sticks requires much greater technique to control the evenness of sound.
  - Practice and learn one section at a time. Do not move to another section until the former section is in a groove.
  - Have students vocalize their parts (not count) to help their learning and aural memory. For example: the first measure of medium drum might be "dag-ga dag-ga." Use higher and lower pitches to differentiate the instruments. Help students learn this concept by having them vocalize the combined rhythms of the three drum parts in section A.
  - Teach *Techno* orally/aurally even though you think it will take more time. Oral learning teaches them to listen and trust their memories.

- Back-up: Bell, Double Bell, and Rattle
  - Have all students learn to play these parts by using body percussion and vocalizing the rhythms.
  - Seat these instruments next to each other.
  - The Double Bell part for section B will require your best players.
  - Ask students to play "on top of the beat" rather than behind. For example, have the rattle players pay attention to their sound rather than when they are hitting the rattle — often there is a slight sound delay.

- Drums: Section A
  - Because all drum parts enter on the upbeat, it is essential that everyone know where the beat is. Start by firmly establishing the beat played by the Bell. You may wish to have students stand and step the beat in place.
  - When everyone is feeling the beat (represented below by a __) in their feet, ask students to vocalize all three drum parts using pitch inflection to differentiate the parts:

    "__ Dug-ga __ dig-gi-dit, dag-ga dag-ga"
  - When they can consistently vocalize all the drum parts, have them continue vocalizing while they start playing their respective drums. Notice that all drums play only high (open) tones.
  - Learning to make up tonal vocal models for their parts is much more musical than counting — a mechanical system driven by reading parts from notation.

- Drums: Section B
  - This is the section that features the High Drum part. Start by having everyone vocalize the part: "Dig-ga-ka-dit dig-ga-dig-ga-ka-dit dig-ga."
  - Medium Drums play the same muted ("mit-ten") tones found in other ensembles. Vocalize and play:

    "Mit-ten da-da mit-ten da-da."
  - Low Drums play hands in pairs. Vocalize the part before playing it.

    "Doom-doom bah-ka Doom-doom bah-ka."

Teacher Tip

Give students a chance to act as section leaders. This will help everyone understand the importance of teamwork.

- Drums: Section C
  - The Medium and High Drum parts are featured here.
  - Medium Drums must immediately start this section with energy .
    Vocalize and play:

    "Da-ga-da-ga-da-ga__da-ga-dat dat."
  - The High Drum part continues what the Medium Drum started. The
    difficult thing for the High Drums is to get in just before the fourth
    beat. Show students how they continue the Medium Drum's third beat.
    Vocalize and play:

    "Dit __ __ ka-dig-ga-dig-ga."
- Drums: Section D
  - This sections belongs to the Low Drum. Teach this part to everyone.
    Carefully observe the right- and left-hand indications. Practice slowly;
    then gradually increase the tempo.
  - Medium and High Drums trade back and forth. Vocalize and play:

    "Dag-ga-dag-ga dig-ga-dig-ga dag-ga-dag-ga dig-ga-dig-ga."
- Leader Bell Signal

  - To change sections a leader plays the following pattern on a loud bell:

  - To signal the end of the piece, the leader plays:

◈ Supplementary Strategies for Techno
- Have students find techno/electronica recordings that work with the
  rhythms in this piece. Play along with them.
- Create four dance sections that can be performed with *Techno*.
- Perform the piece with white gloves or white sticks and black light.
- Have the art
  class create
  performance
  art that goes
  with *Techno*.

Paul Corbiere and students, Boynton Beach, Florida

Wau-Wau Wis-IL

Will Schmid

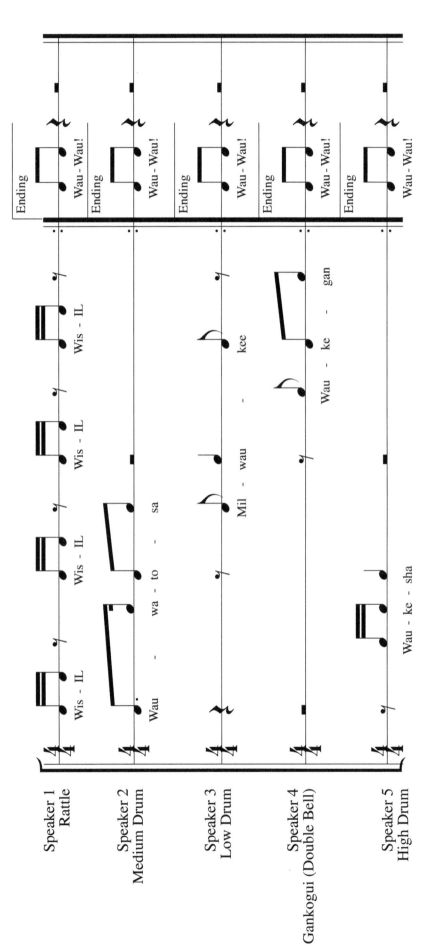

Add solo MC (rap-speaker) improvising over the top of these ostinati using regional place names.

Learning Sequence for Wau-Wau Wis-IL

- *Wau-Wau Wis-IL* is a piece generated from interesting sounding city names from a map of Wisconsin and Illinois. These Native American city names share the common syllable "wau."
- The Performance Idea
  - This piece starts with choral speaking (a style that has a lot in common with rap or hip-hop); then, when all of the speaking parts are clearly established, each part is converted to being played on an instrument.
- Speaking Parts
  - The key to making this sound good is giving each part a distinctive pitch inflection. Nothing could be more boring than delivering this section in a monotone voice.
- Instrumental Parts
  - Each instrument is chosen to represent the type of pitch inflection of the voices.
- Solos
  - Treat this ensemble as a woven background fabric over which students can improvise a rap of place names from the map of Wisconsin/Illinois. A microphone and sound system will give them the power to easily cut through the sound and will also create a cooler performance situation. Instrumental solos could also be played over the instrumental half.

Creating New Map Pieces

- Students will enjoy creating their own pieces based on map place names. Either ask them to bring maps or provide them. This whole activity can be done in about twenty minutes.
- Step 1
  - Students divide into groups of about five or six. Each group should have an assortment of drums, bells, and rattles.
  - Each group starts by looking at their map and finding interesting sounding place names of cities, lakes, rivers, or parks. Write them down.
  - Look at the possible names and decide which ones to use.
- Step 2
  - Use the techniques for Rhythm Complements (composing small group pieces) found in the original *World Music Drumming Teacher's Book*. Play around with the vocal sounds and find ways to combine them in interesting ways.
- Step 3
  - Once the vocal sounds are established, convert the vocal sounds into instrumental parts. Devise a signal for the change to instruments.
- Step 4
  - Find volunteers to speak/rap or play solos over the ensemble. Figure out how to end the piece. Should the piece include movement?
- Step 5
  - Perform the piece for the rest of the class. Do a group self-critique by asking the question: "How could we improve the piece/performance?"

> **Teacher Tip**
>
> *Connect this activity to what is being learned in social studies and geography to help integrate music into the overall school curriculum.*

Supplementary Strategies for Wau-Wau Wis-IL

- Listen to Ernst Toch's "Geographical Fugue."
- Study the relationship of choral speaking to rap/hip-hop, talking blues, and mbira music from Zimbabwe.

Learning Sequence for Interlaken Jam

- Interlaken (pronounced In-ter-lake-en) is the Lake Geneva, Wisconsin resort where we hold our largest of the summer World Music Drumming workshops. One of the evening activities includes jam sessions using Ghanaian xylophones tuned to the C pentatonic scale (C D E G A)

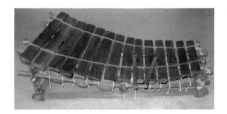

- *Interlaken Jam* can be played with regular classroom xylophones using pitches C D E G A.
  - Build the background parts below in score order.
- Ways for volunteer xylophone (soprano or alto) soloists to take turns playing over the top:
  - Each soloist plays for four or eight bars then turns the solo over to the next person.
  - Soloists play till they are done, and then the next person takes over.
  - Two soloists trade solos back and forth (1 bar, 2 bars, or 4 bars).
  - A soloist plays an improvised call (1 or 2 bars) followed by a made-up response (1 or 2 bars) by the rest of the soloists waiting to play. All of this has to work with the existing *Interlaken Jam* background.
- Solos can also be played or sung using other instruments such as guitars, recorders, or voices.

Interlaken Jam

Will Schmid

Audio Access

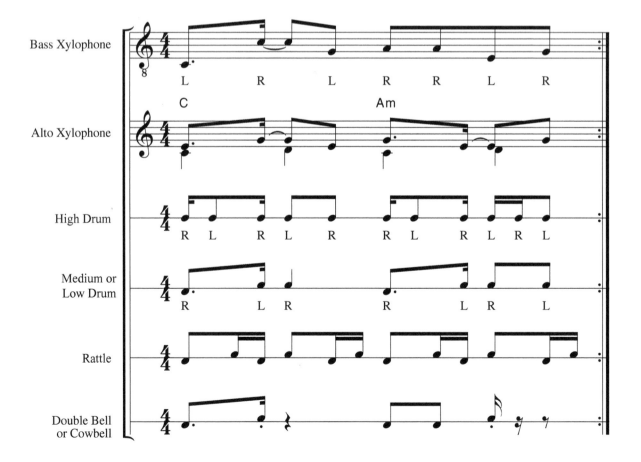

Learning Sequence for A "Player's Dozen" Jam

- *A Player's Dozen Jam* is a piece about the many ways of playing music with twelve subdivisions. Prepare students by asking them how many numbers go into the number 12 (1, 2, 3, 4, 6 and also numbers like 1.5).
- Learn the basic hemiola 3-against-2 pattern first by patting this pattern on thighs:

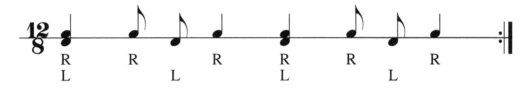

- Now transfer that rhythm to the Bass Xylophone part below.
- Go back to patting the 3-against-2 pattern and vocally subdivide the right-hand quarter notes as eighth notes. This will prepare students to feel the Alto Xylophone part.
- Play the Alto Xylophone part over the Bass Xylophone part.
- Add the Drum and Rattle parts. Notice that the rattle divides 12 into two halves: 3, 3, 2, 2, 2 just like Bernstein's *West Side Story* song, "America."
- The tonality of this piece uses the same pitches as *Interlaken Jam*, but the mode is based on the pitch A and has a distinct minor quality.
- Soloists may play above this basic fabric in the same way they did for *Interlaken Jam*.

Audio Access

A "Player's Dozen" Jam

Will Schmid

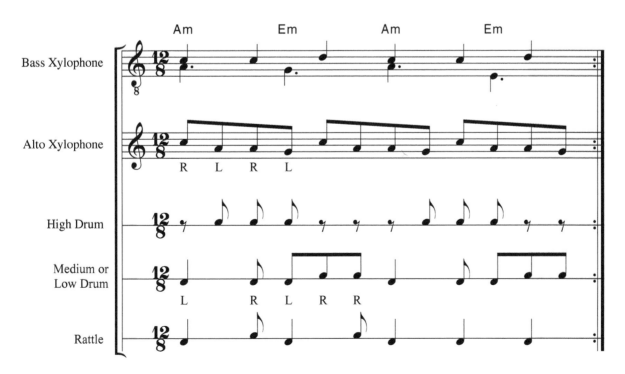

⟨◈⟩ ⟨◈⟩

Recorder Hocket

Audio Access

▦ Learning Sequence for Recorder Hocket

- *Hocket* is a technique for dividing up a melody or composition among players who only have one or two notes. Bell ringers are the perfect example of this process.
- In West Africa it is common to hear both natural-horn and single-note flute hocket ensembles.
- The idea here is to treat the recorder as a rhythm instrument in the same way players have treated drums, bells, and rattles. When only notes in the pentatonic scale are used, the resulting piece created will always sound good.
  – Two easy pentatonic scales to work with on the soprano recorder are:

  G major: D E **G** A B
  A minor: D E **G** A C

- Listen to *Recorder Hocket Sampler* that uses the G major pentatonic notes: D E G A B. Notice how each player plays only two notes over and over in an interesting rhythm. Together the notes weave a fabric of sound. One of the parts is played on alto recorder. A soloist could play something over the top of this ensemble.

▨ Creating New Recorder Hocket Pieces

- Students can create recorder hocket pieces in the very earliest stages of playing. One advantage to this activity is that it provides a rhythmically interesting break from beginning recorder methods that are forced to rely heavily on simple quarter-note rhythms.
- Step 1
  – Students divide into groups of about five or six. Each player should have his or her own soprano or alto recorder.
  – Review the Helpful Hints for Rhythm Complements (at right).
  – Start by finding the notes D E G A B in the G major pentatonic scale.
  – Players should then decide which two notes they are going to play. It is all right for any note to be played in different places by more than one player.
- Step 2
  – Use the techniques for Rhythm Complements (composing small group pieces) found in the original *World Music Drumming Teacher's Book*. Play around with the recorder rhythms and find ways to combine them in interesting ways.
- Step 3
  – Find volunteers to play solos over the ensemble. Figure out how to end the piece.
- Step 4
  – Perform the piece for the rest of the class. Do a group self-critique by asking the question: "What would you do differently next time?"

❖ Supplementary Strategies for Recorder Hocket

- Listen to Herbie Hancock's *Watermelon Man* which begins with an imitation of African flute hocket.

Sound Shapes

Audio Access

Learning Sequence for Sound Shapes®
- Sound Shapes® are a new tool for creating homogeneous rhythm complements.
- Sound Shapes® are simple frame drums that come with a stick. Techniques for playing include:
  - Hitting the head
  - Hitting the frame
  - Using the fingers of the hand holding the frame to dampen the head or change its pitch by pressing on the head.
  - Combinations of the above.
- Listen to *Sound Shape Sampler* that uses four different-sized drum heads. Notice that the players enter in roughly four-beat intervals moving from the highest drum to the lowest. A soloist could also play something over the top of this ensemble.

Sound Shapes®

Creating New Sound Shapes® Pieces
- Start by demonstrating some of the techniques for getting interesting sounds out of the Sound Shapes®. This whole activity can be done in less than fifteen minutes.
- Step 1
  - Students divide into groups of about four to six. Each group should have an assortment of Sound Shapes® sizes.
  - Each group starts by exploring the sounds they can get out of the drum heads.
- Step 2
  - Use the techniques for creating Rhythm Complements. Play around with the drum head sounds and find ways to combine them in interesting ways.
- Step 3
  - Find volunteers to play solos (that could also be played on other drums) over the ensemble. Figure out how to end the piece.
- Step 4
  - Perform the piece for the rest of the class. Do a group self-critique, and discuss some of the different ways groups have produced sounds.

Teacher Tip
*Improvising and composing (National Standards # 3 & 4) should begin with **play time**. If you do not give students time to play around with the instruments, they will take the time anyway.*

Supplementary Strategies for Sound Shapes®
- Investigate the frame drum with stick playing of some of the indigenous people of Alaska or the First Nation people of northern Canada.
- Other interesting homogeneous sources for Rhythm Complements are:
  - Boomwhackers®
  - Miscellaneous junk
  - Kitchen implements
  - Farm tools
  - Wood
  - Cardboard boxes in different sizes
  - Bamboo

Gourds and Boards

Learning Sequence for Gourds and Boards
- *Gourds and Boards* is based on the sound of the many types, sizes, and shapes of gourds (rattles, drums, vessels) as well as wood sounds.
- Listen to *Gourds and Boards Sampler* that uses the a mixture of gourds and wooden sticks/drum shells.

Creating New Gourds and Boards Pieces
- Start by collecting various kinds of gourds, rattles, and interesting sounding pieces of wood. Remember that the shells of drums sound wonderful when hit by sticks. This activity should take about fifteen minutes.
- Step 1
  - Students divide into groups of about four to six. Each group should have an assortment of rattles, gourds, and wood sounds.
  - Start by exploring the sounds that are possible with the instruments.
- Step 2
  - One person in the group starts with an interesting pattern that repeats over and over.
  - Gradually other members of the group find how to fit their sounds into an interesting combination. Use the Helpful Hints in the Teacher Tips box on page 40.
- Step 3
  - Find volunteers to play solos over the ensemble. Figure out how to end the piece. If players are standing, movement with these instruments would be easy to add.
- Step 4
  - Perform the piece for the rest of the class. Discuss the results.

Supplementary Strategies for Gourds and Boards
- Listen to examples of gourd music, "Adenkum/Gourds Galore" (track 3) on Ghanaian Master Drummer Sowah Mensah's CD, *Ntoa (www. sowahmensah.com)*. Sowah Mensah teaches *adenkum* gourd music at the World Music Drumming Lake Geneva, Wisconsin summer workshop (see page 48 for more information).
- Listen to Women of the Calabash's *Kwanzaa* CD.
- Go to your favorite web search engine and find "gourd" or "calabash" sites with a wide variety of information about all types of gourd and gourd uses.
- Slit drums/gongs and tongue drums can also be an interesting addition to the above activity.

Bells and Other Metal

Audio Access

🔳 Learning Sequence for Bells and Other Metal

- Metals produce delightful ringing sounds that have been included in everything from carillon bell towers to wind chimes to Indonesian gamelan orchestras.
- Listen to *Bell Sampler* that uses the a mixture of different sized bells from around the world.

❌ Creating New Bell and Other Metal Pieces

- Stock up on lots of different kinds of bells. Have students bring bells and other metal sound makers from home. This activity takes about fifteen minutes.

- Step 1
  - Students divide into groups of about four to six. Each group should have an assortment of bells and other metal sounds. A variety of beaters from wood to metal should also be used.
  - Start by exploring the sounds that are possible with the bells and different beaters.
- Step 2
  - One person in the group starts with an interesting pattern that repeats over and over. This pattern could serve as the timeline.
  - Gradually other members of the group find how to fit their bell sounds into an interesting combination.
  - Repeat Step 2 several times for different results.
- Step 3
  - Adding a solo may or may not be appropriate. Figure out how to end the piece.
- Step 4
  - Perform the piece for the rest of the class. Discuss the results.
- Step 5
  - Try to create a metal piece with the whole class!

❖ Supplementary Strategies for Bells and Other Metal

- Listen to the middle of "Evening Samba" from the *Planet Drum* CD by Mickey Hart. This all-bell section of this piece is really an ear-opener.
- Investigate the sound of Javanese and Balinese gamelan percussion orchestras. The knobbed kettle bells and gongs from Indonesia produce a clear single pitch as opposed to the splash of pitches in a typical cymbal or gong.
- The *Junk Gamelan* is an activity I once did with 65 people: Build a 2x4 rectangular rack about five feet off the ground (use 12' or 16' 2x4s). Hang pieces of metal that sound good when hit.
  - Position enough chairs for your class around the outside.
  - Equip the players with metal, wood, and rubber beaters.
  - Learn how to play together and improvise a group piece.
  - Chant along with it.
  - Include dancers in the middle.

Bomba güembé

Afro-Puerto Rican

Audio Access

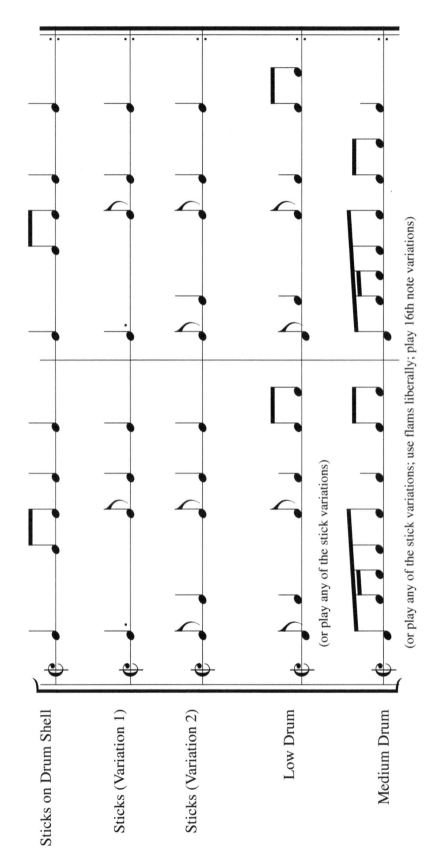

Sticks on Drum Shell

Sticks (Variation 1)

Sticks (Variation 2)

Low Drum

(or play any of the stick variations)

Medium Drum

(or play any of the stick variations; use flams liberally; play 16th note variations)

44

Learning Sequence for Bomba güembé

- Background
  - *Bomba* is an Afro-Puerto Rican secular form of music and dance that has interesting drumming and singing traditions connected with it. Puerto Rican *bomba* flourished south of the mountains and was therefore influenced by the musical traditions of Haiti and the Dominican Republic.
  - The southern singing style typically features a female soloist (call) following by a group of women (response).
  - The bomba drums (*barril*) are large barrel-shaped instruments that are played lying on their side on the ground with the drummer sitting on the drum (like a rider on a horse).
  - The larger drum, *barril segundo,* plays the basic pattern of the type of bomba being played and danced.
  - The smaller drum, *barril primo,* plays elaborations on the basic pattern and improvises conversations with the dancers.
  - *Güembé* is a type of *bomba* dance and rhythm.
  - Listen to examples of *bomba* from the Paracumbé album *tambó*, Ashé CD 2005.
- Low Drum (*barril segundo*)
  - Start by teaching students to play the basic rhythm of the low drum .
  - The Low Drum may also play any of the stick variations using a bass tone at the beginning of each measure.
  - You may wish to have some of your students try playing the Low Drum in the traditional position described above.
  - If you wish to include more drummers, have the Medium Drums join the Low Drum and use High Drums to play the Medium Drum part.
- Medium Drum (*barril primo*)
  - This drum part improvises and elaborates on the basic rhythms.
- Sticks
  - Hit against the sides of the drum shell
  - Several variations may be played at the same time.
- Combining Parts
  - Bring in the parts in score order.

Anne Fennell and Zoom!, Vista, California

Supplementary Strategies for Bomba güembé

- Study other forms of Puerto Rican music such as *plena*.
- If your class or community includes people of Puerto Rican heritage, invite them to share information on their culture with the class.

☑ Performance Sequence for Spirit Drum / Amazing Grace

- Background
  - 19th century English slave ship captain John Newton had a mid-Atlantic conversion while transporting a human cargo from West Africa to the slave markets of the United States. He dedicated the rest of his life to helping to overturn the evils of the slave trade, and he later wrote the words to "Amazing Grace" set to an American folk tune.
  - This arrangement attempts to symbolically restore the drums to the African Americans who were not permitted to play them during the period of slavery before the Civil War (1861-65).
- Verse 1
  - Begin with two measures of Low Drums; then sing verse one over that.
- Verse 2
  - Add Low Frame Drum or Bass Drum and dropped-D-tuned Guitar playing a drone on strings 4, 5, and 6 (similar to the sound of an Appalachian dulcimer with implied one-chord harmony). Sing verse two.
- Verse 3
  - Add Electric Bass playing the lowest string tuned down to D and Medium Drums joining the Low Drums. Sing verse three.
- Repeat Verse 1
  - High Drum join Low and Medium Drums. Audience joins in singing verse 1. Sopranos and tenors sing high harmony part.
- The overall effect
  - Each verse should get louder with a thicker texture.

❖ Supplementary Strategies for Spirit Drum / Amazing Grace

- Study Bill Moyer's *Amazing Grace* video (PBS) for background information.

Spirit Drum

Will Schmid

Audio Access

* Double the Low Drum part on Medium, then High Drums on later verses.

Amazing Grace

Words by John Newton

arr. by Will Schmid

World Music Drumming Summer Workshops

World Music Drumming Level 1

For teachers, counselors, community recreation leaders, church musicians, and players who would like to learn the basics of African and Caribbean drumming, singing, and moving. This course is primarily based on the publications, *World Music Drumming* (Hal Leonard) by **Dr. Will Schmid** (past president, MENC; author). Participants will learn how to implement and teach a course or experience in World Music Drumming. Assisting Dr. Schmid in these courses will be **Sowah Mensah** (Ghanaian Master Drummer, Macalaster College, MN), **Josh Ryan** (Ewe drumming from Ghana and Caribbean specialist, Baldwin-Wallace College, OH), and Teaching Assistants Paul Corbiere, Anne Fennell, Jolene Crowley, Nellie Hill, Margaret Jerz, James Mader, Cindy Mayo and Debbie Montague (experienced school teachers).

The Level 1 class assumes no prior experience with drumming. Those with no background and individuals with prior experience will both benefit from learning how the *World Music*

Drumming curriculum is approached from the very beginning. Because drum ensembles, songs and movement are taught orally, teachers trained in notated traditions often experience a significant paradigm shift.

Daily classes include large group instruction, small group interaction and guided microteaching/leading, and small group ensemble creation/improvisation. You will learn how to drum, sing, move, play xylophones and recorders, and teach and lead others. You will experience strategies for integrating drumming into other school and life experiences, and you will also receive supplemental songs and leader strategies not published in the original curriculum.

World Music Drumming Level 2

For those who have taken Level 1 (or want to repeat Level 2) and want some reinforcement for the original *World Music Drumming* curriculum plus lots of new ensembles, more songs, recorders and xylophones.

This course is based on a review of *World Music Drumming* (Hal Leonard) by **Dr. Will Schmid**, the new *Silver Burdett Making Music 2005* Grades 6-8 (Pearson Scott Foresman), and *World Music Drumming: New Ensembles and Songs* (Hal Leonard). Participants will learn how to improve their teaching and leading of World Music Drumming. Level 2 teachers/participants will also share strategies and materials for using drumming in community contexts such as summer workshops, spiritual settings, adult wellness, and recreation experiences.

World Music Drumming Level 3

For those who have taken Levels 1 and 2 or have <u>significant</u> previous experience in African drumming. Course content will include drumming, singing, and dancing from Ghana (Ga, Akan, Ewe peoples), xylophone ensembles from Ghana, Ghanaian flute playing and Caribbean (Cuba, etc.) drumming, singing. The course content changes somewhat each year and many participants repeat Level 3 a number of times.

Information on the Workshops

For up-to-date information on workshop locations, costs, credit, transportation and other details, visit the website:

www.worldmusicdrumming.com

or write:

Music Workshops, Ltd.
2960 N. Marietta Avenue
Milwaukee, WI 53211

or e-mail:

willschmid@aol.com